New York

974.7

A photographic exploration of how the
city has developed and changed

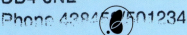

ANNE ROONEY

Chrysalis Children's Books

First published in the UK in 2005 by
Chrysalis Children's Books
An imprint of Chrysalis Books Group Plc
The Chrysalis Building, Bramley Road,
London W10 6SP

ISBN 1 84458 353 8

British Library Cataloguing in Publication Data for this book
is available from the British Library.

Anne Rooney has asserted her right under the Copyright,
Design and Patents Act 1988 to be identified as the
author of this work.

Contact Anne Rooney by e-mail (anne@annerooney.co.uk)
or visit her website (www.annerooney.co.uk).

Associate Publisher Joyce Bentley
Editorial Manager Rasha Elsaeed
Project Editor Leon Gray
Editorial Assistant Camilla Lloyd
Consultant Jeff Lewis
Designer Alix Wood
Illustrator Mark Walker
Picture Researcher Jamie Dikomite

Printed in China

10 9 8 7 6 5 4 3 2

Read Regular, READ SMALLCAPS and Read Space;
European Community Design Registration 2003
and Copyright © Natascha Frensch 2001-2004
Read Medium, **Read Black** and *Read Slanted*
Copyright © Natascha Frensch 2003-2004

READ™ is a revolutionary new typeface that will
enhance children's understanding through clear, easily
recognisable character shapes. With its evenly spaced
and carefully designed characters, READ™ will help
children at all stages to improve their literacy skills,
and is ideal for young readers, reluctant readers
and especially children with dyslexia.

Picture Acknowledgments

All reasonable efforts have been made to ensure the
reproduction of content has been done with the consent
of copyright holders. If you are aware of any unintentional
omissions please contact the publishers directly so that any
necessary corrections may be made for future editions.

T=Top, B=Bottom, L=Left, R=Right, C=Centre
Antiquarian Images: 5R
Corbis: FC C & 9B Royalty Free; 7 Gail Mooney; 19T Lynn
Goldsmith; 22 Bettman; 23 Roger Wood; 25T David Ball
Hulton/Getty Images: 16BR, 18T, 26BL, 28C
New York Historical Society: FC TL, BC TL neg 1047, FC B,
4 neg 73105; BC C, 18B neg 37363; 6T neg 2528; 6B neg
50593; 8L neg 32184; 8R neg 32185; 10T neg 70587; 10C
neg 59171; 10B neg 59167; 12T neg 44117; 12B neg 47587;
14 neg 53661; 16T neg 61741; 16BL neg 33624; 20T neg
1030; 20B neg 46150; 24T neg 48384; 24B neg 51801;
26T neg 32485; 26BR neg 16576; 28T neg 65447; 28B neg
32992
Rex Features: 9T, Henry T. Kaiser
Science Photo Library: 5L CNES, 1986 DISTRIBUTION
SPOT IMAGE
Simon Clay/Chrysalis Image Library: FC TR, BC TR, 1, 2, 3,
11T, 11C, 11B, 13T, 13B, 15, 17T, 17B, 19B, 21T, 21B, 25C,
25B, 27T, 27BL, 27BR, 29T, 29C, 29BL, 29BR, 31

CONTENTS

The land that is now New York was once just swamp and woodland, home to bears and wolves and settled by Native Americans. In little more than 350 years, New York has grown into one of the most important cities in the world.

Then and now

Since the first Europeans settled on the islands of New York in 1624, the area has seen the arrival of millions of people seeking new lives. Some people stayed to become New Yorkers, and the city grew into a centre of trade and industry.

New York also became the gateway to the West. Today, New York is one of the most important commercial and financial centres of the world.

New York City is the largest city in America and the capital of New York State. Central New York is built on Manhattan Island.

Immigrants catch their first sight of the Manhattan skyline, 1934

Time line

10,000 BCE Area first settled by Native Americans

1524 The first Europeans settle in the New York region

1624 European settlers on Manhattan Island found New Netherland

1664 England takes control of New Netherland from the Dutch and renames the city New York

1776 New York declares independence from Britain to become one of the first 13 states

1789 New York declared the capital of America (Washington DC is the current capital)

1886 Statue of Liberty given to New York by France

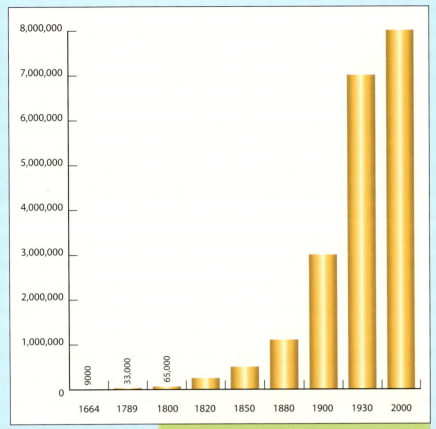

The population of New York has grown from 9000 in 1664 to 8 million in 2000

How to use this book

In this book you will find photos of New York as it was in the past and as it is now. There are questions about the photos to get you to look at and think about them carefully. You may need to do some research to answer some of the questions. You might be able to use:

- encyclopaedias
- CD-ROMs
- reference books
- the Internet.

Page 30 lists useful websites and some films you might like to watch, which show New York at different times.

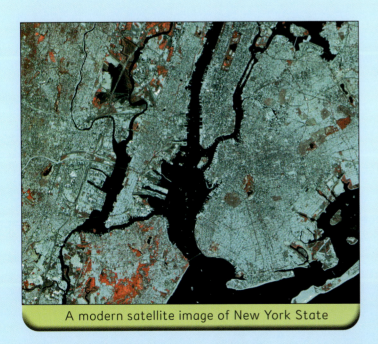

A modern satellite image of New York State

A map of New York dating from 1840

1898 Bronx, Brooklyn, Queens and Staten Island join Manhattan Island as part of New York City

1931–1972 At 381 metres tall, the Empire State Building is tallest the building in the world

2001 Destruction of the World Trade Center by terrorists

1888 A major blizzard freezes New York, killing 400 people

1929 Wall Street Crash and the Great Depression – New York is plunged into poverty as trade and commerce collapse

1972–1974 At 417 metres tall, the World Trade Center is the tallest building in the world

Millions of people have started a new life in America, and many of these people arrived at New York. The Statue of Liberty on Liberty Island has greeted people arriving in New York since 1886.

Famous landmark

- Make a list of the differences and similarities between the two photos of the Statue of Liberty.
- Look closely at the inset photo of Battery Park below. What is different about the sea in this photo compared to the sea in the recent photo?
- In the past, most people coming to America travelled to New York by sea. How do you think they arrive now?
- What can you say about the position from which the two photographs of the Statue of Liberty have been taken?
- How do you think this might reflect a difference in the way that people see the statue as they approach New York now compared to a hundred years ago?

Statue of Liberty on Liberty Island, 1890

Inset: Battery Park with Castle Clinton, 1883

A new life in New York

Today, New York consists of a mix of people from different cultures. Immigrants (people who move from one country to live in another country) leave their homes for many reasons. Some are forced out by famine or war. Others come to provide better lives for their families.

- Why do people arrive in New York today if they are not coming to the city as immigrants?
- Are there immigrants in your neighbourhood, or are you from an immigrant family yourself? Why do you think people would want to move to your area? If you are from an immigrant family, why did your family move?

Investigate

Imagine that you live in a poor country, either now or a hundred years ago. How would you hope your life might be better if you moved to America? What might you regret about leaving your native country?

Imagine that your ship is just coming into dock, or that your plane is about to land, and you are seeing New York for the first time. Write a diary entry of your hopes and dreams for your new life in New York.

Statue of Liberty as seen today

Manhattan has one of the most famous skylines in the world. Architects working in New York aim to create functional buildings that fit in with the distinctive Manhattan skyline.

Limited space

Manhattan is built on an island, so it cannot expand in the same way as other cities. Land must be used carefully. New York has expanded outside Manhattan, but the island is still the central and most popular part of the city. There are many tall buildings in Manhattan as the limited space on the island can be used more efficiently if buildings have many floors.

- How does the Manhattan skyline differ in the old photo and the photo taken in 2000?
- How would it feel different to be on the ground among tall skyscrapers rather than shorter buildings?
- How do you think life in New York has changed as a result of these differences?
- What is the main difference between the two recent photos?

Manhattan skyline, 1876

Terrorist attack

The Manhattan skyline has been transformed in recent years. New buildings have appeared, often hiding or overshadowing those that were once most noticeable. The greatest change took place in 2001, when terrorists flew aeroplanes into the twin towers of the World Trade Center. The attack destroyed the two buildings, and thousands of people died.

- In what other unexpected ways can the appearance of a city be changed so dramatically?
- The World Trade Center was an iconic building that represented the financial success of New York and America. Can you think of a building or an area in your own country that everyone recognises and that stands for something important?

Investigate

Find out about another place that has been seriously damaged by a natural disaster or human act. What was the place like before the disaster? What is it like now? Make a poster or wall display to describe what happened, using pictures of how it was before and after.

Manhattan skyline, 2002

Inset: Manhattan skyline, 2000

P enn Station and Grand Central Station are the two main railway stations in New York. In 1963, Penn Station was demolished and replaced by a modern building. Many New Yorkers objected, and laws were introduced to protect buildings of architectural and historical importance. Grand Central was also set to be demolished, but it was restored in the 1990s in response to public opinion.

Grand Central Station, inside, 1913

Penn Station, outside, 1923

Penn Station, inside, 1911

All change

- Look at the photos of the inside and outside of the new Penn Station and the old Penn Station. What differences can you spot?
- How would it feel different inside the new station and the old station?
- Look at the two photos of the interior of Grand Central Station. How has it changed? What is still the same?
- Which station do you think is the best design for a train station – the old Penn Station or the new Penn Station?
- Do you agree with the decisions to demolish Penn Station and keep Grand Central Station? Explain your answer.

Grand Central Station, inside

Balancing act

Old buildings are often demolished because they are no longer suitable for their original use. A train station may not meet the needs of its passengers if it is too crowded at rush hour or if there are not enough trains to transport passengers. Another problem with a building might be that it is too costly to repair. Planners must think about the costs of repairing a building and keeping it going when deciding whether to maintain an old building.

● What things do people expect to find in buildings today that were not present a hundred years ago?

● Sometimes, buildings are restored but then used for a completely different purpose. Is there a building near you that has been demolished or restored? If so, who made the decision to demolish or keep it? Is the building still used for the same purpose as it was originally designed for?

Penn Station, outside

Penn Station, inside

Investigate

Imagine you were living in New York in the 1960s and wanted to keep the old Penn Station. What would your argument be for restoring the building? Write a letter to the Mayor of New York explaining why you think the old building should be restored.

The area around Fulton Street was once a busy fishing port. When Brooklyn Bridge was built to join Manhattan and Brooklyn (see pages 28 and 29), the fishing industry around Fulton Street died down. The area is now home to piers, shops, restaurants and leisure facilities, but some of the old sailing ships are kept as museum pieces.

Fulton Ferry offices, c.1876

Changing industry

- How has the scene by the docks changed from the 1890s to the present day?
- What is still the same?
- What type of vehicles can you see by the docks, and what are they doing?
- Look at the two buildings in the photo of Fulton Street. How has their use changed?
- Do you think it would be different to walk in Fulton Street in the early 20th century compared to today? Think about the sounds, sights, smells of the area. What type of people would you meet then and now, and what would they be doing?

Sailing ships at the Old Slip, South Street, 1890s

From work to leisure

In the 19th century, Fulton Street was a wealthy area because a lot of trade passed through it. As the fishing industry declined, the area became less prosperous. Fulton Street has since been revitalised by the growth in tourism and leisure activities.

Leisure area and museum ships, South Street Seaport

Investigate

Find out about shipping on the East Coast of America. You could look at passenger ships crossing the Atlantic Ocean, goods being transported between North America and Europe, fishing or whaling. Imagine that you worked in the South Street shipping area as a child and are now visiting it in old age. Write a postcard to a childhood friend to tell him or her about how it has changed.

○ Is shipping still important in New York? How do goods travel to America from Europe and elsewhere?

○ Do you know of any places you can visit that were once used for a particular purpose but are now kept as museum pieces – like the ships in South Street Seaport? What can you learn about life in the past from places like this?

Pier 17, Fulton Street

Railways were very important in America a hundred years ago. They provided the only easy way of transporting goods and people across the country. Early trains were pulled by steam locomotives. They produced a lot of smoke and were very noisy. Most modern trains are powered by electricity and so are cleaner, quieter and much faster.

Take the train

- How do the trains in the old photo look different from modern trains? Can you still travel on trains like this? Where?
- What do you think you would notice if you were standing in Grand Central Rail Depot in 1905?

- Which types of transport can you see in the recent photo of Park Avenue?
- Today, the railway tracks are hidden from view underground and the trains leave Grand Central Station through a network of tunnels. Why do you think the railway was not built underground in the first place?

Grand Central Rail Depot, 1905

Transport today

Today, there are many different forms of transport, and more people travel today than in 1905. Many goods people buy, such as clothes and food, have also been produced a long way away. As a result, more transport is needed.

- What methods of transport are used to move goods and people now?
- How has the development of new types of transport affected people's lives?
- Make a list of the advantages and disadvantages for people and for the environment of travelling by train compared to other methods?

Investigate

Imagine you have to take a journey between two cities in America. Find out how you could travel. How long would it take to travel by each method? How much would it cost? Which would you prefer? Imagine taking the same journey in 1905, when you could only travel by train. How long would the journey have taken? Make some tickets for the trip, showing the departure time, the arrival time and the cost.

Park Avenue, looking towards Grand Central Station

The ways in which people and goods are transported around the streets has changed a lot in the last hundred years. This has affected the environment and daily life. Before bridges and tunnels were built to cross the Hudson River, people could only get to New York by ferry.

George Washington Bridge, c.1932

Road users

Road transport falls into three different groups – people walking (called pedestrians), private transport and public transport. Private transport, such as bicycles, cars and lorries, are used by individuals. Public transport is for everyone to use and includes buses and trains.

- How are people moving around in the old photos of the street scenes below and left?
- What types of vehicles can you see and what are they used for?
- What new type of transport is shown in the photo from 1925?
- Are the pedestrians behaving differently in the photo from 1925 and the recent photo?
- Can you spot any differences in the two photos of the George Washington Bridge?

Broadway seen from Barclay Street

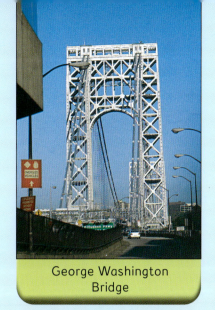

George Washington Bridge

Cars in the city

Today, more people have their own cars than they did in 1925, when the old photo of Fifth Avenue was taken. In the old Broadway photo there are no cars, and wealthy people are travelling in horse-drawn carriages. Tradesmen delivered goods using horse-drawn carts.

- What do you think is the best way of travelling from one part of New York to another today? Think about private and public transport methods.
- How have the changes in transport affected the environment and people's lives?
- Do you think it is healthy to walk on the street today?

Investigate

Conduct a survey to find out how people in your class travel to:

- school
- shops
- distant friends or relatives.

How many different methods of transport are used? What types of transport are used most for long journeys and what types for shorter journeys?

Draw a bar chart to record your findings.

Intersection of Fifth Avenue and 42nd Street, 1925

Broadway

17

Today, most people spend less time out on the streets than they did in the past. A hundred years ago, most people walked to the places where they worked or visited. Many people also worked on the streets as tradesmen, either selling from a market stall or moving around selling their goods from a barrow.

Fifth Avenue at 50th Street, 1902

Shopping on the street

- Look at the photos on these two pages. How does the clothing of the people differ in the old and recent photos?
- Can you tell whether people are rich or poor by the clothes they are wearing?

- Where are people shopping in the old and recent photos and what are they buying? Where do you think it would be easier to shop?
- Are there any places we can shop now that look like the earlier pictures? What sort of places? Are there any near you?

Junction of Hester and Norfolk Street, 1898

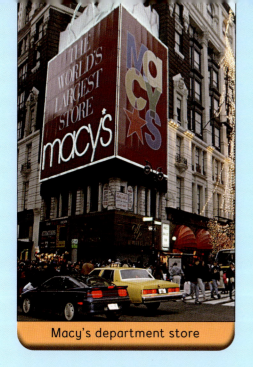

Macy's department store

Streets of change

Today, there are many street activities that are not shown in the photos on these two pages. If you walked around a modern city, you might see street performers entertaining people, people sitting in cafés and people asking for money.

- Have the activities people do on the street changed since the old photos on these pages were taken?
- In the past, people used to visit several different stalls or shops to get their shopping. Have supermarkets, department stores and Internet shopping changed the ways in which people shop and what they buy? How has it changed the lives of people who sell goods?

Fifth Avenue from 60th Street

There were many poor people in New York a hundred years ago. Most had just moved to the city and lived in wooden shacks lining the Hudson River. Space is still in short supply today, so most New Yorkers now live in apartment blocks or have moved from the city to the suburbs.

Fifth Avenue at 16th Street, 1892

Rich and poor

In the past, wealthy people lived in expensive houses built on broad avenues. These people often had servants, who usually lived in the same houses in small servants' quarters on the top floors.

- What is different about the areas in which rich and poor people live in the two older photos?
- How would the local community in each old photo differ from the community in which you live?

- How does your community differ from those shown in the recent photos?
- What sort of area is Riverside Drive in the recent photo? What are the buildings used for? Can you tell whether it is a wealthy or poor area?

Riverside Drive, late 19th century

20

Fifth Avenue at 16th Street

The housing gap

Very often, rich people live in large apartments in smart areas, and less wealthy people have smaller apartments in less popular areas. Some areas that were used for housing are now used mainly for business. One example is Fifth Avenue, which has changed from a residential area into a busy shopping district.

- How has the change from houses to apartments allowed more living space to be created in New York?
- What types of houses are common in the area in which you live? Do people live close together or far apart?
- In New York, more land has been created by draining nearby swamp land. In other countries, land has also been created by developing farmland, fields or forest. Find out about the changes in land use in your own country and somewhere with a very different natural environment.

Investigate

Imagine you have just moved to New York in 1890 and are living in a shack on the banks of the Hudson River. Write a letter to your family describing where you live and what it is like. Include a picture showing what you have inside the house.

Riverside Drive

Many people in America were wealthy in the 1920s, but banks were lending too much money, and people were spending more than they could actually afford. Following the 1929 Wall Street Crash, America was gripped by poverty in a period known as the Great Depression. Many people lost their jobs and homes, even people who had been very rich.

Gripped by poverty

During the Great Depression, many New Yorkers had to queue for free food at soup kitchens set up by charities and businesses. They lived on the streets or in makeshift homes made from scraps of wood and old boxes.

- How are the men dressed in the photo of the soup kitchen below?

- What kind of food do you think was served in a 1930s soup kitchen? What type of food is being sold in the recent photo?
- What is the old man in the recent photo doing?
- Who do you think is helping the men in the soup kitchen? Who might want to help the old man outside the fast-food outlet?

New York soup kitchen, 1930s

Helping the poor

The amount of help, called aid, given to poor people around the world varies. Some countries provide a lot of help, but others cannot afford to do much. Very poor people often depend on aid for survival.

- In what kind of circumstances do you think people need help? Think of personal events and any recent national or world disasters.

Many people from developing countries live in severe poverty. Families often grow their own crops, and a drought will take away their only food supply. Millions die each year as a result of famine and disease.

- What should the governments of wealthy, developed nations such as America and Britain do to help these people? What can you do to help?

Investigate

Make a soup kitchen meal at home. You will need day-old bread to eat with it. Get help from an adult to make the soup from scraps of meat and vegetables such as potatoes, carrots and onions. There were rarely fresh vegetables for soup kitchen meals so you will have to use old vegetables. Invite some friends to your soup kitchen, and see what they think of your meal.

Hot dog stand on Broadway, 1960s

Central Park is a huge area of green space in the centre of New York. As well as trees and grassed areas, there is a large boating lake and the Metropolitan Museum of Art. Many people use the park for sports such as running, tennis, horse riding and cycling.

Skating in Central Park, 1913

Central Park

The land used for Central Park was once a swamp. When it opened in 1857, it was the first public park in America.

- What different leisure activities are people enjoying in the photos on these two pages?

- Do you think these activities have been organised as public events, or do you think people have just decided to do them on their own?
- What differences do you think you would notice about what it is like to be in Central Park now compared to what it was like at the times the older photos were taken?

Central Park, 1894

Aerial view of Central Park

Public gardens

Most New Yorkers live in apartment blocks and do not have gardens. Central Park is an important space where they can relax outside. There are lots of events to enjoy, such as open air concerts and sports events.

- Is there a public park near your home? How do people use it? Do you use it yourself? Carry out a survey of people in your class to find out who uses parks and what they do there.
- What type of leisure facilities are found in public spaces near you? Have they been there long?

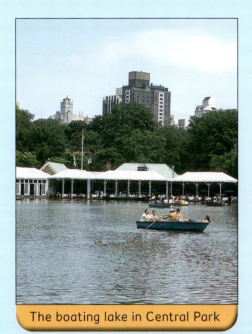
The boating lake in Central Park

Investigate

Find out a bit about the history of Central Park – what people can do there and what it is like – and then make a leaflet that could be given to visitors. Look at leaflets about attractions near you to get some ideas. Your leaflet might include a map of the park. You could include advertisements for events, for things you can buy in kiosks there or for activities you can do.

A concert in Central Park

In the last hundred years, many parts of New York have been redeveloped. Some have changed so much that they are no longer recognisable as the same places.

The Polo Ground at Fifth Avenue and 110th Street, 1886

Changing places

The Waldorf-Astoria Hotel moved from Fifth Avenue in 1929, and the Empire State Building took its place – then the tallest building in the world. Lennox Avenue was once a busy area where wealthy people lived. Later, the area became associated with crime, and people moved away. New businesses have started to move back in, and the area is improving. Some time before 1957, the Polo Ground at Fifth Avenue moved to 155th Street. The site of the old arena is now a cheap residential area.

- Look at how each of the places in these photos has changed. Why do you think that these places have changed?
- How do you think that the changes may have affected the people who lived in these areas?
- Can you think of any places in your local area that have changed recently?

Lennox Avenue, 1930

Waldorf-Astoria, c.1900

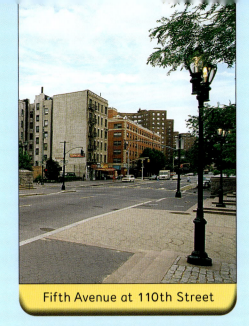
Fifth Avenue at 110th Street

Investigate

Try to find an area or a building near you that has changed dramatically in the past few years. Imagine you have been asked to make a radio or television programme about it. Write a plan for the programme, and find out the information you need. You might like to ask the local residents about the area or building before it changed. Why was the area changed? What was it like while the changes were taking place? How did it affect the local residents? You could even make your radio or television programme as a class project if you have a tape recorder or video camera.

Location and lifestyle

In the past, homes and businesses could be found in the same parts of New York, but they are now usually separate.

- Are there areas near you that were once used for housing but are now used for something else? What has happened to the people who used to live there?
- Where do people in your local area live, shop and go to enjoy themselves? Are there large shops and leisure areas in the centre or are they further away?
- How are people's lives changed when the places they need to visit are spread over a large area?

The Empire State Building

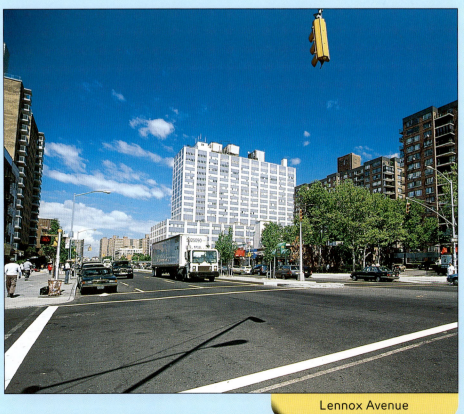
Lennox Avenue

Some parts of New York have changed very little. St. Patrick's Cathedral was completed in 1888. When work started, the building was situated outside the city centre. When the cathedral was finished, it was well within the city centre because New York had grown so quickly. St Patrick's is the largest Catholic church in America. It is modelled on medieval European cathedrals. Jefferson Market Courthouse was also built to resemble a medieval building.

Jefferson Market

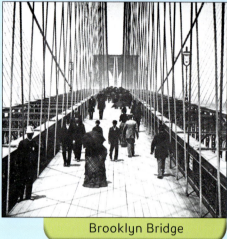
Brooklyn Bridge

St Patrick's Cathedral

Crossing the river

Brooklyn Bridge opened in 1883. The first people to cross it were very nervous because the bridge sways in the wind. A separate roadway runs below the walkway.

- Why do you think that St Patrick's Cathedral has not changed?
- In what ways are the photos of Brooklyn Bridge different?
- Do you think these structures will change in the next hundred years?
- What reasons can you think of for changing places such as these?

Keeping it the same

If a building is still used for its original purpose, and there is no major structural damage, there is often little reason to change it. Often the outside of a building can stay the same.

- Have the ways in which churches are used changed? What about other places of worship, such as mosques and synagogues?
- Do you think people's expectations of places of worship have changed in the last hundred years?
- Why might a bridge need to be changed?

Are there any places in your local area that have not changed for more than a hundred years? Choose a place you know that has not changed, and find out when it was built and what it is used for. Is it likely to carry on being used for the same purpose?

Jefferson Market

Brooklyn Bridge

Investigate

Imagine how the place where you live might change in a hundred years. Draw a picture of how it might look in the future. What do you think will have changed?

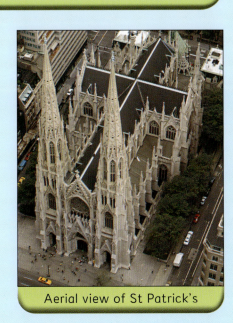
Aerial view of St Patrick's

St Patrick's Cathedral

29

On the map

This map shows where the places photographed in the book are in New York.

1   Battery Park (page 6)
2   Broadway (pages 16, 17)
3   Brooklyn Bridge (pages 28, 29)
4   Central Park (pages 24, 25)
5   Empire State Building (pages 26, 27)
6   Fifth Avenue (pages 16–21, 26, 27)
7   Fulton Street (pages 12, 13)
8   George Washington Bridge (pages 16, 17)
9   Grand Central Station (pages 10, 11)
10 Jefferson Market (pages 28, 29)
11 Hester Street at Norfolk Street (pages 18, 19)
12 Lennox Avenue (pages 26, 27)
13 Macy's department store (page 19)
14 Metropolitan Museum of Art (page 24)
15 Park Avenue (page 15)
16 Penn Station (pages 10, 11)
17 Riverside Drive (pages 20, 21)
18 South Street (pages 12, 13)
19 St Patrick's Cathedral (pages 28, 29)
20 Statue of Liberty (pages 6, 7)
21 Waldorf-Astoria Hotel (page 26)
22 World Trade Center site (pages 8, 9)

At the movies

There have been lots of movies set in New York. To get a glimpse of life in old New York, watch:

King Kong.
Directed by Merian C. Cooper and Ernest B. Schoedsack, 1933.

Metropolis.
Directed by Fritz Lang, 1927.

For recent New York, watch:

Inspector Gadget.
Directed by David Kellog, 1989.

Muppets Take Manhattan.
Directed by Frank Oz, 1984.

On the Internet

A set of postcards of old New York:
http://lsb.syr.edu/projects/postcards/index2.html

Take a tour of New York, with lots of images of the city as it is now:
www.nycmap.com

Find out about the buildings of New York:
www.emporis.com/en/wm/ci/bu/mf/?id=101028

Find out about Grand Central Station:
www.wordiq.com/definition/Grand_Central_Terminal

Find out more about Central Park:
www.centralpark.org

aid help given to people who live in poor countries

blizzard severe snowstorm

cathedral large church

commercial relating to trade

declare state officially

demolish to pull down or destroy

drought period of no rain

famine severe shortage of food

ferry a boat used to carry passengers and vehicles across water

financial relating to money and finance

functional designed for a particular use

Great Depression period of poverty and failure in trading during the 1930s

iconic standing for something

immigrant person who has come to live in a country from elsewhere

independence being separate or free from the control of something else

leisure time time spent enjoying yourself

locomotive a railway engine

makeshift put together from whatever materials are available

medieval from the Middle Ages, the years 500–1550

mosque Muslim place of worship

overshadowing towering over

pedestrian person who is walking

poverty having little or no money or basic resources

residential relating to places people live

skyscraper very tall building

suburbs the residential areas near or outside the edge of a city

swamp an area of soft and permanently wet ground

synagogue Jewish place of worship

terrorist person who commits criminal acts to make a political point

tradesman person who sells something or carries on a trade

INDEX